Why Do You Stay?

BY: ELIZABETH JAMES

This book is affectionately dedicated

to

Bonnie

Contents

Chapter 1

Why Do You Stay?

I've been considering asking you this question for years. It's a question I don't want to ask, but it's never far from my thoughts when we're together. We've been dear friends, or a sister, your mother, or a daughter so I feel I know you well, but there is a situation surrounding you which concerns me greatly. I'm aware of your predicament because I have been beside you, and at other instances viewing from a distance, watching it get worse over the years. Time passes slowly when you're married or in a relationship with the wrong person. I wonder to myself, *why do you stay with him?* It's been years, the relationship hasn't improved and you're still there. Perhaps for your situation as the reader of this book, the duration of the relationship has only been months, but you know it's not working. Isn't it great that you can leave anytime you wish yet . . . you don't? You stay.

During my first interactions with him, I would notice little things said by him to you, here and there. He was on his better behavior in the beginning, because he wanted to manipulate me, as a person close to you, just as he slowly maneuvered you. I did what most people do when they notice bad behavior in adults they are getting to know, I laughed it off while I'm with you. But you are my friend and it's not okay to demean you in front of others, even a little bit.

He shows glimpses of his true self when he thinks no one is around to see. When he walks in from work, not realizing I'm in the kitchen getting myself a drink out of the fridge, not in his line of sight, and he yells at you after asking what is for supper. No matter what your answer, he finds fault with the suggestion and tells you he wants something else. I walk out of the kitchen, smiling, ignoring the outburst, saying hello. He knows I heard the entire conversation then I see him back peddling trying to say what a hard day he had at work. Always an excuse for his bad behavior.

I know he doesn't like me. It's all over his face. He knows I know who he really is. I say nothing to him. It's not my place. But I want to tell him to take a hike, leave you alone. Two minutes of time is all I would put up with his controlling behavior. No one deserves to be treated like this . . . well, no one but him.

He's not always this bad. Just sometimes. Although more lately. You make excuses for him.

See the situation as it really is. Look at your treatment by him as if you were watching a television show. You would turn the channel because watching someone being verbally abused is difficult to watch. Get out now. It will not get better. Why do you stay?

Chapter 2

I'd Like to Have Known You Before

I can't imagine what you would be like, without the millstone that is him around your neck. Your life as a child, a teenager and young adult must have been filled with hopes and dreams like everyone else. Working hard through school to develop a career where you would thrive and excel. You are smart and would've succeeded and climbed the ladder in any profession if only you were not held back by an individual who could not have his spouse more successful than he. You tell me how he belittles you in front of others and makes fun of your accomplishments when you're alone to puff up his ego. This impresses no one. Does he not know how this makes him appear to others? He truly doesn't care. All that is important at this stage is pulling you down. We know this because he does it in public to embarrass you in front of others, and in private when no one is watching and paying attention but you.

When we are young, we have so many plans. Plans for our life, for our career, for love, for a family and a home. We all know it is a better idea to date an individual for a couple years to truly see the good and the bad. But sometimes we fall in love, and we fall hard. Love is powerful when you find yourself in its grip.

Jumping in quickly may work out if you are lucky and a fortunate soul, but you could also find yourself with a shark pretending to be a dolphin.

Making the wrong choice for a companion is easy to do when they know the right words to deceive you. It can happen to any of us. We all makes mistakes. When I was in college, I had a dear friend who was deceived. Her boyfriend, let's call him Frank, checked most of the boxes; handsome, charismatic and charming, a doting boyfriend and he gave all of us the impression he cared for her. My boyfriend at the time would tell me little things he noticed when he was alone with Frank, just the guys, and specifically on one occasion, the weekend before they were to be married. When pretty women would walk past him, he would flash his smile, say hello in a flirty sort of way and give them a look which conveyed for her to come and get him later. This one instance struck my boyfriend as odd for a man who was about to get married in two days to a young lady who in her own right had been a former beauty queen. My boyfriend knew she was my dear friend and was concerned enough about the situation to tell me about it that evening. I dismissed it as Frank was still being a flirt which we all were aware of this. At her rehearsal dinner the next night, she told me her father had pulled her aside and told her she still didn't have to go through with the wedding. He wasn't convinced of Frank's devotion to her and feared for her future happiness. She kissed her father and told him not to worry so much. She knew Frank was the man for her and everything would work out. I did not tell her about what happened with Frank while my boyfriend was with him. She had convinced me that Frank was truly devoted to her and would be a loving and caring husband.

The wedding went on as planned the next day with no hiccups and my friend and her husband prepared to move to a large metropolitan city several hours away to begin new promising careers for both of them. We wished them well and told them we would stay in touch which is something you say to one another even though you live a thousand miles apart. Keeping in contact with friends who live a considerable distance apart was much harder to do before we all had cell phones.

I forgot about the newly married couple except for fleeting thoughts of my friend, wondering how she was getting along in the big city, until my boyfriend who had since become my husband ran into him at a mall in our town a year later. He was shocked to see Frank since they had moved to another city so far away. My husband looked around for my absent friend and asked Frank where she was. Frank stood still a moment with a disappointed look on his face and said that she had left him. My husband, in unbelief, asked what happened. Frank proceeded to explain that he had cheated on her with several ladies and once his wife had walked in on him while he had another woman with him at their house. My friend packed her clothes and left that day. She had her other things removed from their apartment within the week.

Unbelievably, Frank was now upset with himself and said it was the biggest mistake he had ever made in his life. He said he had tried to convince her to give him another chance, but she refused and was moving on with her life. She got her own apartment and had remained in her job moving up the ladder quickly. Frank on the other hand, had lost his job and moved back in with his parents. My husband said he almost felt sorry for him due to his life crumbling around him, but it was all due to his own actions. My friend had not allowed an individual to remain in her life who did not respect her and treat her with kindness and dignity. She knew she deserved better as we all do.

The one positive side about messing up is most of the time, you can right the situation. All of us have been duped in one way or another and when it involves love, we are all vulnerable. We assume the individual we are dating will treat us in a manner as we treat them. We think they would not knowingly inflict harm on us or take advantage of our trusting nature. I'm sorry to tell you, that is not the case. Everyone must be mindful and pay attention when you are dating. People cannot hide who they really are for long. Their real personalities peek out at random intervals and you cannot dismiss what you see and listen to what others are telling you.

The longer you spend with a person who is mistreating you, the less time you will have to find the person who values your company. Not many choices during our lifetime, lasts for a lifetime. You are not tied to him with a chain. Why do you stay?

He keeps getting passed up for promotions. Work is really tough for him right now. I will focus on me when he gets settled.

He will never be settled. The time for you is now!

Chapter 3

Who Could You Become Without Him?

I see your potential pouring out with little effort on your part, unable to hold back the force that is future you until he comes around and it becomes muffled. You are held back by his remarks, his actions, his glances in your direction. He will not tolerate you excelling around him. From an outsider observing, you are not even trying to outshine anyone, it's just you being who you are inside. A gift to the world in whatever you do, whether it is medicine, shop clerk, farming, teaching, fast food or blogging, whatever you are called to do, you are finding your way . . . and you cannot get to who you were meant to be with a partner who brings you down rather than lifting you up.

Perhaps you are a young woman spending time with a young man in a relationship that started out good. It's been several months now, or perhaps a year or two, and you've noticed there are more and more conflicts. Arguments are increasing or even worse, maybe you don't like to argue so you go along with his demands, but you are unhappy. Something inside is whispering to you to get out. You tell yourself, *but it's not all bad*, so you stay. What you cannot see, is how the good times are only good when you go along with his wishes.

Perhaps you are middle age, with a partner of 20 years, and it has been a struggle for the last 15 years. You have been complacent, allowing bad behavior, just to keep the household calm, trying to prevent one of his outbursts but he finds an excuse to shout when he finds one item is not in its right place. Looking back, he has never treated you as his partner in life. You are simply the one who provides extra income for the household, fixes the food, cleans the house and completes whatever extra tasks he requires of you because he's too busy with his pastime interests. None of the regular household chores you complete does he show appreciation for you providing. As far as he's concerned, it's your job to keep the house neat and see to his every whim.

He shows his attitude toward you when he flirts with random attractive women with whom he comes in contact except for the confident women who he would never choose because he knows she would put him in his place for being inappropriate. You will notice he always flirts with women who do not know him. They are strangers reacting to someone saying something nice to them. He does this because women who really know him do not want to accept a compliment from this man. They know what he's trying to do, and they want no part of it. This is all a show put on by him, for you to witness his appeal to others and how lucky you are to be in his company. More manipulation.

Perhaps you are a senior citizen woman who has been married for 40 years, you have a home, a car, nice things but his behavior toward you is off-the-scale cruel. He doesn't even hide his contempt for you now, even when you try to do everything he asks. It is never enough when it is from you. When he wants you to do extra for him, he knows how to turn on the charm and make you laugh so you see glimmers of the man you knew in the beginning, back when you were dating him and your whole life lay before you. Your potential was and still is unlimited. Time has moved forward but you have not. You have stayed in this dead-end relationship with a person who does not value your thoughts and wishes, ever. No matter what you say in conversation, he tells you what you just said is ridiculous and he wants to correct your interpretation. No matter what you do, it's wrong. He has to show you how it's done correctly. No matter what you are interested in, he tells you what a waste of time and just leave the ideas on ways to spend your free time up to him. All of his treatment of you is unacceptable.

No matter what your age or gender, you deserve to be treated kindly with understanding. If you are not, you need to change your circumstances. Why do you stay?

He struggles without me. He doesn't realize he needs me.

He has always seen your potential and it scares him. He should be happy for you and want you to soar.

Chapter 4

Have You Ever Known True Love?

So, what was he like when you first met him? Was he sweet, romantic, ever dotting with his full attention? Did you like how he took care of you, made sure your needs were met, protected you and made you feel safe? There are signs when someone is putting on a show for our benefit. What he's telling you does not make sense with what we see with our own eyes.

Most of the time, there will be little hints of truth showing themselves if you are being deceived. There are many instances when a person who verbally abuses their partner may also be cheating on them. They do not respect the relationship so it's easy for them to make the leap to cheating. He told you he would be at work on the weekend but why would he be there nearly every weekend. Or is he working overtime most evenings but not coming home acting like he's been at work for 16 hours? Perhaps on occasion, you notice he should've been at work or somewhere else in his routine. If he is someplace out of his routine and he did not invite you to go along, beware. The fox is on the prowl. He may not be cheating but most likely, he is. And if he's not, he's still doing something he should not be doing and he's hiding it from you. Perhaps it's gambling or drugs, any option hidden by your significant other is betrayal.

You may even find yourself in a warped reverse situation of the fox slipping around where you find yourself hiding your everyday activities from him because he is so controlling. You're sitting at your computer reading your daily emails, clicking on sales or the latest YouTube video. He walks by and says, "What are you looking at now?" in an irritated tone. You click out of the sight and turn off your computer to avoid a fight instead of saying what you really feel. This behavior reinforces his control and you find yourself closing your computer when you hear him stirring in the other room. Tell me, why you can't look at your computer and read your emails when you feel like it, not only when he is out of the room.

Do you get a package in the mail for yourself and hide it? Does he get agitated every time something arrives for you and not for him? I am not talking about a situation where someone over spends online and puts the couple's finances in jeopardy. Just normal purchases when something is needed for yourself whether it be clothing or cosmetic. Does it upset him when the package is for you and not for him? He gets so distressed because he is not controlling your every move. You are making purchases without consulting with him first even though you are working and paying for it yourself. You begin wondering whether you should make your purchases when you need them, or should you risk his wrath and another outburst. You convince yourself you will be able to get to the package first and open it before he sees it.

If his treatment of you had started out this way, you would have quickly shut the relationship down. But over time, you have come to accept this behavior as normal in your relationship. It is not normal. Both parties should treat one another with love and respect and be able to talk out any differences to find common ground. No one deserves to be controlled ever.

True love is caring. It is kind and patient. You want to be with the other person even when you have nothing to do together. Just to be around them. Whatever you are doing, washing the dishes, taking out the trash, mowing the grass, watching a movie, reading a book, you wish they were there beside you, helping or not, just being with you. A person *really* in love is not rude or harsh, conceited or dismissive, demanding to always have their own way. Love is helpful to one another, giving their partner the benefit of the doubt when the whole story has not yet revealed itself. Love is truthful, you never have to worry, it never deceives. Love is funny. You laugh at one another constantly, even when it's not that humorous. When you're with your partner, little things they do strike you as funny and you chuckle just thinking about them. Love is not suffocating or unselfish. You want your loved one to be free to do what makes them happy, even if it's not something that makes you happy. Love is enduring, it does not wash in and out like the tide. It will happily be with you until the end of time.

So, again I ask you. Have you ever known true love? If you have only had one serious relationship and it is with the controlling jerk you are with now, the answer is no. That is not true love. True love is unselfish, giving, humble, just and supportive. Why do you stay?

Because I know a nice person is in there.

He's manipulating you with his words, so you will ignore his actions.

Chapter 5

Betrayal/ Lies

You had no idea he wasn't working overtime at the office. The thought never entered your mind because it's not something you would do. His friends cover for him during the weekend or anytime he needs an alibi. You would've never found out if someone had not seen him and told you about it. Thank heaven for friends who tell you the truth even at the risk of upsetting you.

When his phone would ping, he would scramble to get look at it before anyone else had time to react, then just as quickly, he would close it out and give a quick dismissal as one of his friends goofing around. When you would later ask to see his phone, he would quickly say, "You don't trust me," or something to the effect of life being so difficult living with a distrustful person such as you. Simply put, he tells you your suspicions about his guarded reactions is all in your head. It's your fault. Then you start to question yourself. Am I being too suspicious of his behavior? Should I not want to look at his phone?

This is all a ploy he uses when you are getting too close to recognizing the truth. He makes a grand jester of how over-the-top your questions are toward him and the louder he gets the more he's deflecting. Anything to turn the attention away from the matter at hand, his deceit.

It's not only his betrayal by cheating. It is also his betrayal to you by his reaction to a normal question that would be no reaction if something hidden wasn't really going on. Betrayal in effect, by not treating you like a normal person with normal curiosities reacting to odd behavior which cannot be uttered for fear of an overreaction. This causes you to begin tiptoeing in areas you should be allowed to walk in and walk out of with no elevated response. Again, you begin to wonder what truly normal behavior is because you do not live with a normal person.

What really confuses me is why this abusive person stays in this toxic relationship rather than leaving with the new girlfriend. If he would leave, he wouldn't need to hide his behavior any longer. Perhaps he knows the new girlfriend would send him out the door with his suitcase if he treated her this way or maybe he's is a twisted individual who simply enjoys tormenting you by seeing how much he can get away with or maybe yet, he knows he is better off keeping you around, dangling at the end of a string, only engaging with you when it is beneficial to him. Whatever the reason, you deserve better. Get out now.

Why do you stay?

Sometimes he's really funny and we have a great time. I just never know which personality I will get each day but they're not all bad.

Wouldn't it be wonderful to be with an individual who never hid other relationships from you?

Chapter 6

Money & Control

Are you living with a sponge? Between the two of you, you were always the one who was good with money. You never overspent and could turn twenty dollars into one hundred with your different investments. Property was purchased because of you, then a house built, children entered the picture, a home was created, and a comfortable life began. Yet his paycheck was never deposited into the household account. It was always you paying the mortgage, utilities and buying groceries. He would contribute some money on various months for groceries or utilities, but you always had to ask him for it.

He never chipped in for the payment on the mortgage, always throwing up to you that it was your idea to buy the property and house. He never volunteered his fair share of household expenses although his name is on half of everything you purchased. In fact, when the time came to purchase the property, he didn't really want your name on the deed, but you insisted. He tried to create a scene in front of the realtor to keep you quiet but thankfully this time you spoke up. After all, you did find the home and wanted to purchase it. He always told you he would've been content to continue renting. He went along with putting your name on the deed with his, but you knew you would have to listen to his little comments for six months of how you needed to have your nose stuck in every decision that was made for the family which is untrue. A characteristic common with a verbal abuser is they can spew any nonsense out of their mouth, whether it makes sense or not, as long as it is tearing down their significant other.

Here we are years later, and he still keeps his money separate and he's still continuing to sponge off you without contributing unless asked. Not putting your income together was always fine with you, many couples live this way. But they also both voluntarily contribute to the cost of maintaining the household. It's understood by both parties.

You try not to ask for his share anymore because it always produces an argument resulting in him telling you, there would be no problems if you would only manage your money better as he does. This is him still trying to get control of the money you have earned. You tell him he's not paying his fair share and he imitates you saying this like a child would do on the playground with his friends in kindergarten. He does this because he has no reasonable comeback that makes sense. He knows he's not paying his share, so he must deflect away from the topic again.

The only financial situation worse than living with a sponge is living with a sponge who has control of both your finances. If you have given control of your finances to a controlling individual who is not forthcoming with information at the end of each month and has poor communication skills in that they do not like to be questioned about their care of the finances, even if it's money you have earned, you are in a perilous predicament.

First and foremost, you need to take back control of your money. You need to sit down with your partner and have a serious discussion about your finances. If he does not want to have this discussion, then tries to manipulate you by playing the guilt game, saying you do not trust him. Or perhaps he plays the anger-guilt game and explodes, yelling and screaming then saying, "That will be the day when you control his money", even if you only asked to share the chore of managing the household finances.

If you find yourself in either of these two examples of money control, and you cannot take back your share, you need to exit this relationship as quick as possible. There is no repairing the situation by communication, control of your finances must be taken back. This may be difficult if he has complete control of your finances. Do not let on to him as you take steps to gain control by opening a new checking account and moving your direct deposit to that account.

Finances in a loving and caring relationship can be worked through and decisions made to benefit both individuals. Having one person in the relationship handling the finances works fine for many couples when there is proper communications between the two individuals and both parties are involved in the paperwork, getting a summary of spending at the end of the month. This can work really well if there is good communication between the two as you can discuss goals for your spending such as retirement, children's education and perhaps a vacation house.

If you cannot communicate about finances with one another and you are paying the majority of the household expenses or the other individual is demanding control of both finances with no accountability, this is not acceptable.

If the communication is broken down to the extent you cannot have a conversation about your combined finances or your finances alone, this is huge red flag concerning the relationship. Hopefully, you have not let his control seep this far into your financial life. But be weary. A controlling person is manipulative, and they will move in slowly, taking control in one area first, then before you realize it, he's controlling another area, then another. If you are a person who likes to please, it is easy to be caught off guard.

Why do you stay?

He tells me how much better he is handling money than me. Maybe he is. But I still never seem to have enough to pay the bills.

You're paying for everything now. Why not take back control of your money and really know what is being spent.

Chapter 7

Verbal Abuse

I'm aware my perspective is different from yours. Putting up with him for one minute longer than this very moment right now would not be an option for me. Steps would be in motion, today, to begin removing him from my life.

Your kind and forgiving spirit allowed his behavior to start small and grow into this horrible stench that is his daily verbal abuse. You recognize it now because his behavior is so bad and encompasses your nearly every waking moment depending on his mood. He treats you civil and will sometimes throw in a better-behaved day as long as you do everything he wants. It's when you want to do something to improve the house or you try to choose the restaurant, or you buy something you want to wear or use, then the verbal abuse starts up.

A package comes in with your name on it without his knowledge you placed an order, no matter how small, it starts. You fixed something for dinner without his approval first, he's not eating it. He tells you to throw it in the garbage. After an hour, he storms in the kitchen saying he's hungry and to fix him the list of items he wants. You want to go out and eat at the new restaurant in town. He resists for several weeks, then he says okay. He's going only because you want to, but he tells you he thinks it's a bad idea. Then, no matter how good the food or the service, he says it is the worst food/service he's ever had, and he will never go back there again. You need to know, it's only because you picked the restaurant and it gives him another chance to lash out at you. Or like the time all of us went to the local Italian restaurant which is a versatile menu where everyone can find something they like. He placed his order and announced that the two of you would be sharing a meal because there was too much food in one order. I thought to myself, *what if she doesn't want what he is eating for her meal?* You said nothing to correct him. You went along so as to not start an argument out in public. Even if you would have only corrected him, saying you would like something different, he would have made a scene, raising his voice, telling everyone you never finish your meal and what a waste of food and money.

This is his MO. He doesn't have any apprehension to tear you down in public or to embarrass you to get you to do his will. He will make you out to be the one who falls short no matter what the situation. Even if he makes a mistake, he announces to everyone in the room, it was because of your action that he made the mistake. Implying if you were not in the picture, no mistake would have been made. What is so scary, is it takes energy to be this mean to a person. It takes thought and action, planning and calculation. He seems to do it effortlessly, like it's his first reaction to choose the option that is worst for you.

The reader of this book must think, *Can anyone truly be this evil and manipulative for no reason? What is their endgame?* Each situation has their own set of reasons. My belief in this case of observer which I've found myself in, is he's jealous of who she could become. He knows his shortcomings therefore he must hold her back or she will rise to who she was meant to be and that is not to be with a person who does not value her as an individual. If she would become who she was meant to be, she would kick him to the curb and share her life with another who loved her and wanted her input on how to spend their life together. If only she realized she would not be alone because she has family and friends who support her and will see her through this trying time. Then again, this reason for mistreating her maybe giving him too much credit by suggesting he has a reason. A person who is this evil to another human being could just be an angry, manipulative, poor excuse of a human life who wants to mistreat others. They are out there. More than we'd like to believe. Why do you stay?

I'm sure there are worse people out there. What if I end up with one of them or alone?

You will not be fooled the next time. You have experienced the warning signs and the results of inaction firsthand. You will see them coming immediately. As far as you being alone, this will never happen as long as you have friends and family. It's easy to expand the friends list. Just get involved in your community.

Volunteers are needed everywhere. You will have plenty of choices for activities on whatever evenings you wish to fill.

Chapter 8

To All the Young Ladies

(Or Young Men)

You are still in your youth with maybe your 20's or 30's ahead of you. You cannot use the excuse, you have too much time invested with this individual and cannot start over in a relationship (which is a ridiculous path of thought because you are never too old to put up with abuse). Does he/she ask you where you have been when you didn't answer their text? Are they critical of your words or statements? Does he/she overreact to normal situations? Does he/she discourage you discussing ways to improve your current situation or give you reasons why not when you tell him/her your hopes and aspirations? Does he/she show little interest in what interest you?

If you answered yes to any of these questions, you need to give serious consideration to cutting ties with the person you're with. An individual who does not want you to pursue your dreams in a responsible manner does not value you. Do not let the relationship continue as it will only get worse not better.

Remaining with an individual who does not respect your opinion or value your input in a conversation or in decision making is absurd. This does not prove how great your love is for him/her, that it can overcome all obstacles. It is merely a power trip for the individual in that they can mistreat you anyway they please, and you will stay.

If you have spent some time with the person you are with and have a optimistic outlook toward them, there is a tendency to overlook red flags warning you this may not be the person for you. We all tend to ignore red flags in our relationships and let bad behavior infractions pass because most people are overly understanding and know everyone has bad days. But let's think a minute back to your last bad day. Did you lash out toward your loved one or friend? Most of us will say no. We simply wanted to forget about the day and do some other fun activity to get our mind off whatever ruined the day for us. Yet, when you are mistreated by your significant other, you make excuses for them, *He had a bad day at work,* and you trust him because you have history together, *He's a respectable person. He wouldn't want to do something to hurt me.* After trust is built with an individual, it is normal to overlook small infractions of your partner, but this is when it's important to pay attention. Is it starting to happen over and over? Are the small infractions growing larger and the blame pointing to you?

Are you being isolated from your family or friends? Does he make comments when the phone rings, *That's probably your mother. I wonder what's wrong now?* When he makes comments like this, you find yourself actually dreading the phone call with your mother. Or maybe he sits in the same room with you while you're on the phone only to blast you with questions about the conversation or tear down your friend who just called. *She brings all this drama on herself because she runs around too much with her friends. She should spend more time at home and mind her own business.* He's hinting to you how you need to be home with him more and not visiting with your friends, so you won't end up like your friend. This is an isolation tactic used by him to maneuver you with his comments. All of this is manipulation to get you to behave in a manner he wishes and restrict you to not behave as you wish to do. And you're making the choice to remain home and not visit or talk to your friends and family to please him. Again, this manipulative behavior by your significant other can creep up on you and before you know it, you're changing how you react to your friends and family without even knowing it. Because you're trusting and you assume the best of the individual you're with and look over the worst.

If you stay too long with an individual who is controlling, then attempt to cut ties with him, he may go into a blind rage and do something drastic like killing you and sometimes himself. Get away before it's too late and you get in too deep. This is all too common and has happened many times before. The key to getting out is to recognize the behavior early and leave before the verbal abuse escalates and the physical abuse begins.

Maybe you're thinking, *He is controlling and dismissive of me, but not to the level of constant indifference and violence.* My response to you is good for you, but now is the best time to go. If you wait until the behavior is common and every day, it will be more difficult to remove yourself from the relationship.

My mind goes to the 2021 case of Gabby Petito who was strangled by her boyfriend while traveling across the United States in a van. She was young to recognize the signs of controlling behavior exhibited by her boyfriend as dangerous to her well-being. This can be difficult to identify in the beginning of a relationship due to the calculating and cunning conduct of the verbal abuser. He knows how to hide his behavior from others and make you feel like it's in all made up in your mind alone.

What we know of the abuse inflicted on Gabby by her boyfriend, Brian Laundrie, begins with the Moab police conducting a traffic stop of the couple, after a 911 call had been received reporting a man and woman in a white van with a Florida license plate who had been arguing and the young man shoved the young lady and slapped her. A short time later, the police located the van driving erratically and signaled for the vehicle to pull over. When the police approached the car, Gabby began explaining why she was presently crying, then she immediately took the blame for his erratic driving by saying she was distracting him (she blamed herself). When the police officer separated the couple, Gabby proceeded to tell the officer she had OCD and was cleaning the van and she had been apologizing to her partner for being so mean (blaming herself). Further into her explanation, she told the officer her boyfriend had locked her out of the van until she had calmed down (he's controlling the vehicle thus the trip). She was visibly shaken over the whole ordeal, so the officer put her in the back of his air-conditioned vehicle while he took her boyfriend's statement. (I am curious to know if she was diagnosed with the OCD disorder by a doctor or did her boyfriend tell her she was OCD which she took as truth).

When the policeman walked back to approach the van, the boyfriend who was still seated asked the officer if he had spoken to his fiancé, Gabrielle (his way of letting the policeman know they were to be married). The officer asked him to step out of the car and proceeded to ask him what was going on. The boyfriend, in a calm composure, immediately started blaming Gabby for starting a fight and stated that he was only trying to create distance between them until she could calm down which was why he took the keys and locked her out of the vehicle (all her fault). He then went on to say Gabby had grabbed the wheel which was why he hit the curb while driving (again, blaming her). The officer asked if she had her foot on the gas too, since he was driving over the speed limit. The boyfriend said no, that was from the adrenalin due to the police lights and her grabbing the wheel that caused him to speed up (again, not his fault). He then proceeded to tell the officer that during the disagreement, he wasn't pushing her, only pushing her away from himself (she was the aggressor). The officers decided after interviewing both parties that Gabby was the aggressor and her boyfriend was the victim. Gabby did not defend herself and took the blame, her boyfriend blamed her for the entire dispute and accepted no responsibility. How are the officer's supposed to react to this? Are they mind readers? Can we blame them for not saving Gabby? Did they not know how some abused women are so beat down mentally, they take the blame for their abuser's bad behavior? Thirteen days later would be Gabby's last social media post, her body was recovered a little less than a month later, ruled death by strangulation by the coroner. A little over a month later, her boyfriend's remains were found after killing himself, leaving a note, saying killing Gabby was a mercy killing after she had experienced an accident and was in so much pain, he had to strangle her to relieve her suffering (still not accepting responsibility, even at the end of his life).

This is why, especially, young ladies, you need to be diligent in recognizing the signs. Verbal abusers, even the ones you have been involved with for some time, are master manipulators and if you are not watching, they will slip into your life long-term before you know what's happening.

Moms or Dads, if you are reading this, make sure your daughters are able to identify the behavior of beginning verbal abuse. Talk to them before they begin dating so they will be able to recognize abusive behavior early on in the relationship. This is not a natural subject for us to talk about with our children because as parents, you assume your daughter or son will not put up with improper behavior from their significant other. But we must remember, love relationships are new to our young people. They may not be sure what is acceptable norms and what is not. They are used to dealing with individuals who are looking out for their well-being such as parents and teachers. Dating an individual who confesses their undying love for them can cause a young person to alter their normal behavior. They could tolerate unacceptable behavior because they trust the individual who says they love them.

Parents must be clear in their communication to their teens and young adults of what constitutes a healthy supportive bond between two people. If your teens or young adults see controlling behavior from their boyfriend or girlfriend, give them the knowledge to put a stop to it immediately and the mental strength to break off the relationship before they are past the point of being emotionally strong enough to move on. It is easier to have this conversation with our teens before they are in a relationship. Drawing attention to a partner who is attempting controlling behavior toward your daughter or son during a relationship can push them toward feeling the need to defend the individual. Make sure they know better is out there and they are worth it.

Chapter 9

Signs of Verbal Abuse

Your boyfriend makes a comment which hurts your feeling and it's happening more and more lately. Now is the time to self-assess the treatment you are receiving. When you tell him, what he said did hurt your feelings, does he apologize, or does he tell you to stop being so sensitive and continue the barrage.

Let's take a few moments to examine some signs of verbal abuse from a companion or spouse. No couple gets along flawlessly but when you care for one another, you don't want to mistreat the other. Everyone goes through periods when emotions get heated and tempers flare but just as quickly you regret what you said and tell your significant other, you're sorry. At the other end of the scale, when you notice a temper which seems to rage much more often by one spouse or partner, it's time to reassess this relationship.

Waiting for the bomb to drop during conversations – Do you find your self tip-toeing during conversations? No matter what you say, he yells at you, telling you how wrong you are or turns around what was said to mean something completely different than you intended. You find yourself now becoming super aware of everything you say or do, so as not to be the trigger to set him off. This is your way of trying to limit the amount of verbal abuse you take. He will try to

34

convince you; his anger is caused by your behavior or something you said rather than taking responsibility as being someone with overly controlling characteristics who cannot even control his own outbursts. Then when you try to not engage him in conversation as much to limit the outbursts, he yells at you for not talking or ignoring him. This is when you usually get called some kind of name such as a backward animal, or perhaps an inanimate object such as a rock or stump or even something much worse.

Constant Verbal Criticism – Have you noticed you can never do anything right as far as he's concerned? How you spend your free time, he criticizes. The supplements you take to stay healthy, he says they are a waste of money. How you exercise, he says the technique is you're using is not correct. Don't get me started on your cooking. The food is never right, even when you fix everything just as he has always taken it. Now he wants the potatoes chopped thinner or the soup was too thick. The fried apples were not sticky enough or the bacon is undercooked. His demands have increased over time to the point that you feel as though you cannot accomplish any task well. Your self-esteem has plummeted over the past years to the state you find yourself constantly apologizing for things you do correctly which your friends and family instantly pick up on. They ask you, *why are you apologizing all the time.* They know why, do you?

Shouting and Yelling or the Silent Treatment – On the few occasions when you stand up to him, you notice the situation quickly escalates to yelling. At this point you must be careful as the verbal abuser could cross over into threats and even physical abuse. When you make this small step forward of briefly standing up for yourself, it triggers a shock reaction on his part and he knows you must be quickly jerked back in line. He yells and screams, calls you names, mimics you and talks over top of you so you find yourself yelling to be heard. After the yelling and threats by him are over and things have calmed down, the abuser may try to pass off their behavior as a one-time thing or they are under stress brought on by work or perhaps you. Again, they mention their bad behavior is caused by you.

Also, after the yelling and screaming, he may use the silent treatment just to let you know there are consequences to standing up to him. It's strange that he recognizes behavior from you which he doesn't like (such as standing up to him) then he punishes you for it, but you do not hold him accountable. He can treat you as terrible as he wishes, and you are still kind to him. His silent treatment does not last long because he doesn't want you to stop waiting on him. If he's not talking to you, he can't order you around or tell you all the things you are doing wrong. He does use the silent treatment though as a punishment and make no mistake, it is a form of verbal abuse. He holds back the joy of his companionship from you, which in his mind, is a terrible consequence.

Humiliating Comments to Others – Have your friends told you how he talks about you behind your back? It would have to be a really close friend or family member, otherwise people tend to keep quiet and stay out of the fray. He mentions little things you do which he exaggerates so it will appear he's not nit-picking. What is really disturbing is how he mentions things to me, someone in your circle, about how messy you are or how you are constantly slipping food and eating it behind his back. I ask him why he doesn't pick up whatever he finds messy in the house. I suggest him helping out more. He gets quiet when I suggest this then he makes excuses for why he's too busy to help out. I don't discuss with him, you slipping and eating food because I know why you do this, you don't want to be criticized for eating whatever it is. If he is telling me these things, what is he saying to your face if he catches you snacking or worse yet, what is he telling the people who are his friends. He's a top-notch manipulator, even with his friendships. His goal is to turn your friends and his friends against you. He's trying to isolate you which gives him more control over you.

Everything is Your Fault – Have you noticed how every argument he starts gets turned around to be your fault? A verbal abuser is constantly playing the victim, all-the-while tearing down those around him. You try to defend yourself by explaining what you were doing is nothing to have an argument over then you're told it's your behavior that is causing the argument and they are the one who must put up with you. This results in the verbal abuser blaming you for their over reactions which causes you to think less of yourself and have a lower self-esteem.

Warning Signs of Beginning Verbal Abuse – Failure to Accept Responsibility After an Argument - Does your partner or spouse dismiss your feelings after a disagreement? Whatever distress you may have about the subject of the argument or the argument itself which resulted from an overreaction to you bringing up a conversation they did not want to have is quickly rejected by the abuser. They tell you you're recalling things wrong and if there is any reason to be upset it is them because you caused the argument. They Raise their Voice - Does the conversation quickly become loud when there is no reason to yell? If this happens more than once, you'd better pay attention. Moments of Extreme Anger then Extreme Kindness - Does your partner blow up one minute, calling you names, tearing you down, maybe even threatening you, then the next day they are complementing you, being overly kind and caring, trying to subconsciously convince you there was no bad behavior which previously took place on their part.

Why Do You Stay?

No one else would take care of him like I do.

It's funny you feel this way, even though he talks to you like it would make him happy if you left today. *He doesn't talk like this all the time.*

Chapter 10

He's Kinder to the Dog

You know he has the ability to treat people with kindness because you see how well he treats the dog. He takes care of his animal with a level of attention to detail that amounts to him caring more about this animal than anything else in his world. I can't help but think, it would be nice if he spoke to you in the same soft-spoken tone he speaks to the dog.

Anyone would appreciate that level of adoration. When the dog gets a cough or itch in the ear, he runs it to the vet. When you go to the physician for a new dark spot or newly noticed lump, all you hear is "Why are you always going to the doctor? There's nothing wrong with you." He buys the dog new harnesses with a matching collar, memory foam bed and the best food available. When you buy a new blouse, his first response is not "That is nice. It will look pretty on you." It is always, "What did you get me?"

Perhaps, if you would behave more like the dog, he would treat you better. You could say nothing when he is around, just look happy when he talks to you. Sleep most of the day, hang out in the yard on occasion, digging in the flower garden (not necessarily planting, just digging weeds) or watching the birds fly by.

You go back inside when you're thirsty and need to get a drink or a bite to eat. Do you think that would be a better life? If you say yes, Why Do You Stay?

His treatment of the dog shows you he has the ability for compassion and kindness to others . . . but only for those who obey his commands and who cannot talk back.

Chapter 11

Everyone Knows . . . He's Fooling No One

Deep inside, you hope no one notices. He puts on his little show of a wonderful life to others. He charms, laughs, cuts up with passer-by acquaintances, especially the opposite sex who are attractive. His goal is to put forth this picture of what a wonderful person he is and how crazy you are.

There are those who are around him, from a distance who buy his charade. They do not spend enough time around him to see the real him slither out. But there are your close friends who are with you every week who see his true self. Most do not mention the situation to you but be sure they do know what is happening.

Verbal abuse on another cannot be held in by the abuser for an extended period of time. If he is with you while in the company of others, his behavior will show itself over and over. The abuser can turn it off for short periods but not when you come in contact with others daily or several times throughout the week. It's too confusing for him plus he cannot be good to you for an extended period of time. Any situation, where you are involved, he must demonstrate his control over you. He doesn't want you getting any wild ideas like you make your own decisions where your life is concerned.

Sometimes, when he is out in public, and he thinks no one knows him, he may not hide his verbal abuse of you. Strangers will see him yell at you, demean you in public and they will look in the other direction. Those who fear for you may speak to you when he steps away to see if you are alright. Others may call 911 and report the abuse if it becomes especially heated such as in the Gabby Petito case.

I was watching from a distance when your significant other was especially hateful to you in a mall on one of our weekends together. As your partner stormed off angry, I walked up to you just as a passerby who also had witnessed the outburst approached. He leaned in close, so you would hear his whisper. *Do you want me to go bust that guy in the mouth for you? No man should speak to a lady like that.* You answered, *No, just ignore him* but I remember thinking that was what he deserved, to be called out on his behavior of you. Maybe not a bust in the mouth, we don't condone violence on either side, but called out that his treatment of you was not acceptable

Why do you stay?

I know I should go.

Leave him. You deserve better.

Chapter 12

So, Why Do You Stay?

Time for some real soul searching. I want you to read this chapter slowly and carefully and answer the questions truthfully. No more pretending. No more ignoring the facts. Are you with an individual who is tearing down your self-esteem, calling you names, raising their voice and this is a big one, blaming you for their bad behavior? When you try to talk with them about your concerns, do they dismiss you and tell you your imagining things and overreacting? Do they manipulate you by guilting you into staying in the relationship when you know what is best for you is to get out?

You know deep down how you're being treated. No more excusing his or her bad behavior toward you. It has been my experience when an individual mistreats their partner in an overly controlling manner, the behavior does not improve. They either become more controlling or they resent you even more for sticking up for yourself.

Some victims of abuse say they stay with their abuser because they are afraid of them. They are fearful of the reaction when they tell their significant other they are leaving. Wanting to avoid a confrontation is something all of us strive for but just the fact you are fearful of his response is evidence enough there is a real problem with this relationship. The longer you stay in this verbally abusive relationship the further slanted your perspective will become. You will struggle to even recognize his treatment of you is abusive. The behavior will feel more normal as time goes on, then before you realize it, you cross over into that area of your abuser being unwilling to let you go without harm.

Only you can change your situation by making a decision right now and acting on that decision. I know it's scary. There are so many variables. Will he explode in a tirade of name calling? Probably. Will he tell you how all this arguing is your fault and will improve if only you would act better towards him? He most definitely will. Will you be alone sometimes when you would normally have him to accompany you to an event? Most likely there will be those instances, but you have friends and family and can make arrangements for them to be there for you.

You must remember, you are removing yourself from an individual who does not value you. Recognize he is toxic and you deserve better. There will be no more getting loud, blaming, criticizing and demeaning you. You must remove yourself from him to move on to bigger and better. Recognize now that he is toxic to you and it's time to change your situation.

So, ask yourself the following questions: When I am with my significant other, do I alter my behavior to prevent them from criticizing me? Do I go along with how he/she wants to spend their free time to prevent criticism? Do I find myself wanting to check with them before I make a decision to prevent a later confrontation? Have I noticed no matter how many suggestions I make for places to eat, vacations, watching TV, etc., they are always rejected? Have I noticed after every argument, nothing is ever settled? Does your significant other always have very good excuses for their bad behavior? If they can justify the bad behavior in their mind, they will never change it.

If you have answered yes to any of the previous questions, you are in a verbally abusive relationship and you need to get out. The longer you stay, the harder it will be to leave. After you are free from them, you will wonder why it took you so long to get away, so you can, at last, breathe again.

Life is hard enough without spending time with an individual who does not value you as a person. You are an amazing person who has their own special gift, unique to you, with much to offer the world. Stop wasting your gifts by remaining with a tyrant. Take off your blinders, pull the tape off your mouth, feel your confidence building inside, untie your feet, get up, begin walking then break into a run and start living.

Why do you stay?